Fritz and Balthazar

Their adventure with tree spirits

by
Bodo Henningsen

Pictures
Petra Jakob

Translation
Klaus Buring & Team

Copyright: © 2016 Bodo Henningsen
From German into English: Klaus Buring & Team
Cover and setting: Erik Kinting

Published by tredition GmbH, Hamburg

All rights reserved. No part of this publication may be reproduced, translated, distributed, or transmitted in any form or by any means, including photocopying, recording, or other electronic or mechanical methods, without the prior written permission of the publisher and author.

On a clear autumn day, **Lou** the owl was doing as she did almost every day: sitting fast asleep, hidden in a crook of a branch.

The old oak tree in which **Lou** lived was still full of leaves, so it really was an ideal hiding place. As usual, there was heavy traffic on the main road which skirted the area, but the creatures who lived there were used to it.

But suddenly a new sound grew louder and louder and eventually settled over the tree with an enormous roar.

It felt like a hurricane. The thinner branches of the oak bent and shook. Almost all of the leaves blew away. **Lou** huddled closer to the tree trunk as the hurricane ruffled her usually immaculate plumage.

Now, through the suddenly naked branches, **Lou** could see a helicopter above the tree in which there were three people: the pilot, the co-pilot and the boss of the highway planning department.

The boss was saying "To straighten out this road here, all we have to do is remove one old oak tree!"

The pilot replied: "And then you could build a rest area where the bend used to be."

The helicopter turned and disappeared, and silence returned. **Lou** laboriously groomed her feathers and closed her eyes. Two jays landed on top of the tree and wondered why almost all of the leaves were lying on the ground. Usually they knew everything that happened near the edge of the forest, but they hadn't noticed the helicopter.

Soon life in and around the oak tree returned to normal.

Deep inside the old oak lived **Big Cloud**, the old spirit of the tree. He had lived there from the very beginning.

All of the animals as well as the many younger tree spirits in the forest called him **Big Cloud**. There was a reason, of course: every time he took an extra deep breath he looked exactly like a huge cloud of fog. Even though he usually slept during the day, he had once played a joke on **Jack** and **Cracke**, the two jays, by making the tree disappear in a big cloud of fog in broad daylight, so that they could not land after one of their patrols. This was **Big Cloud**s way of punishing them for constantly disturbing his sleep during the day with their loud screeching.

And then, in the spring, it happened. A family of mice who lived under the tree was industriously hunting for food when a heavy jeep turned from the road into the meadow and drove toward the oak.

All the mice ran in panic to their mouse holes and disappeared underground. All, that is, except one.

This was young **Fritz**, who had once again been playing alone, away from all the others. **Fritz** was different. You could recognize him even from afar, because the tip of his tail looked like a paintbrush. He had injured it badly in an accident and it had grown back just like a paintbrush. All the other mice teased him about it constantly, and because of that he usually kept himself to himself.

As well as this, **Fritz** had a cheeky-looking snub nose and exceptionally big, dark brown button eyes.

As **Fritz** was rushing towards the mouse hole, the jeep stopped right on top of it, covering the entrance with one of the wheels. **Fritz** was too late and would have been squashed if he hadn't stopped as fast as he did. Shocked, he ducked behind a wheel and wondered what would happen next.

Two men and a woman got out of the jeep and immediately started to unload things: red and white stakes, measuring equipment, a table and three chairs. They rushed back and forth with their instruments until they decided that they had planted enough stakes in the ground.

Fritz watched it all carefully, but didn't really understand what was happening.

Then the three people grabbed something to eat out of the jeep and made themselves comfortable at the table. **Fritz** sneaked closer to them and hid behind a basket so that he could listen to the conversation.

Just then the driver of the jeep said "As the planning inspector, I'm very happy that we can start building this road. Now all we have to do is get rid of this old tree. It's right in our path."

The woman, a surveyor, who together with her assistant had put all the stakes in the ground, replied: "You know, it's really a pity about this old oak. All this, just to make it easier for people to drive like maniacs."

A thunderstorm was approaching, and so the three people quickly packed everything into the jeep and drove away, leaving behind two rows of red and white stakes. Between these was the old oak tree and of course **Fritz**, who first ate all of the scraps that had fallen from the picnic table and then disappeared into the mouse hole to escape the pouring rain.

Deep inside the mouse hole the family was very happy and relieved when **Fritz** arrived unharmed. They made him tell them exactly what he had experienced and what he had heard.

"We mustn't let that happen!"
"But what can we do?"
"And who can help us?"

„Hey! Let's ask **Lou** the owl, she's the wisest one here", suggested **Fritz**'s sister. But then **Balthazar**, their great-grandfather, signaled that he wanted to speak.

"And which one of you wants to go to **Lou** the owl? In the past, relatives of ours have gone to her for advice in times of crisis, but the emissaries never came back! You see, she is a little too fond of us …
as food!"

Sadly, and at a loss to what to do, the mice decided to sleep on it in the hope that they could come up with a solution for the problem the next day. **Balthazar** went outside beside the entrance to the mouse hole and looked up at the moon as if it could tell him something. From the edge of the forest he could hear the calls of **Lou** the owl, who was out there hunting mice.

"No", said **Balthazar** to himself. "You really couldn't ask her, it would be suicide!"

While **Balthazar** was sitting there contemplating, a big cloud rose up into the sky and drifted in front of the moon.

"I've got it!!" **Balthazar** yelled suddenly. "**Big Cloud**! I have to tell our tree spirit what the humans are planning on doing with his tree!"

The tree spirit had lived in the old oak as far as anyone could remember and all the animals of the forest knew him. He had already been there when they arrived. During the day he mostly slept in a hole in the oak tree. He was really ancient, and the many younger tree spirits in the forest had a lot of respect for him. Now and then he would attend when they met at midnight in the big clearing.

The old tree spirit naturally had all the arts and crafts that a real spirit needed. **Big Cloud** could make himself small and transparent so that nobody could find him. He could change his color. If he was really upset he would become a dark reddish purple. If he was happy, he would take on a wonderful, delicate bluish-green color. But his most famous skill was when he would take so deep a breath that he would become a huge cloud of fog. Yet because it was so exhausting for him to do this, he hadn't done it in a very long time.

The younger spirits would always try to imitate him and even went so far to organize competitions like "Color-Changing" and "Spirit-Expanding".

Balthazar waited until it was midnight and then ran to the hole in the trunk of the old oak. *Big Cloud* had just awoken and warmly welcomed his visitor. His eyes glowed bluish-green. When *Balthazar* saw that, he knew he was welcome there.

"Greetings to you, **Balthazar**, old friend! It's nice of you to come and visit me. But surely you must have a special reason for being here."

"I am afraid I have, **Big Cloud**", started **Balthazar**. Our little **Fritz** has found out that the humans have terrible plans, They want to cut down our old oak tree and bring the road here.
"They can't do that!" exclaimed **Big Cloud** as he listened to **Balthazar** explain the whole story to him. **Balthazar** finished by pleading, "**Big Cloud**, we don't know what to do. Only you can help us."

"Of course I'll help you. Remember, this is about my home too. First I'll have to talk to **Lou**. I'll will ask her to convene a meeting with the tree spirits tomorrow in the big clearing. There, you and **Fritz** will tell everyone everything you know."

Balthazar was shocked. "That's much too far for **Fritz** and me. Plus we have to pass through **Lou**'s territory, and what about the fox?
We'll never get there alive!"
"Don't worry", said **Big Cloud**. "I will talk to **Lou**. I will make sure that she gives you safe passage through her territory.

As for the fox, he won't see you if I escort you there. So, please, come tomorrow at midnight."

Balthazar thanked him profusely and hurried back to the mouse hole to report everything to his family, and especially to **Fritz**.

Meanwhile, **Big Cloud** floated out of the hole in the tree trunk and wandered in and around the old oak looking for **Lou** the owl. He found that she had just landed on the most comfortable branch of the tree and was eating a freshly hunted mouse.

"Hello **Lou**, old friend! I hope that is not a member of **Balthazar**'s family!"
"No, no, **Big Cloud**, you know how much I like a peaceful life!"

Big Cloud shrank his head down to approximately the same size as **Lou** and radiated a greenish glow. He then sat down comfortably on the branch beside **Lou**.

"Do'nt mind me. Just keep on eating", he said, and then told **Lou** the terrible news.

Lou was also shocked and immediately promised to help them, as the old oak was her favorite tree as well. Naturally she too had seen the red and white stakes.

After they had talked about everything, *Big Cloud* asked *Lou* to come to the meeting and give safe passage to *Fritz* and *Balthazar*.

"Of course! Tell them both that they have nothing to be afraid of!" said *Lou*, and then flew away to invite the tree spirits to the meeting that was planned for the next night at the witching hour.

Big Cloud floated back to his tree hole and lay down to sleep. During the night, he dreamt horrible things of felled trees and monster diggers. It upset him so much that he actually changed color in his sleep and turned red and purple. The bat who lived above him in the hole was terrified when he saw him like that.

Meanwhile **Lou** was on her way, inviting the tree spirits to the meeting. Her repeated calls echoed eerily through the dark woods.

She had almost no time for her nightly mouse hunt, so she was tired and hungry when, just as dawn was breaking, she arrived back at her sleeping-place in the old oak tree.

Balthazar told his family about his successful arrangement with **Lou**.
Nevertheless they still had a restless night and ended up with a very early morning start to look for food so they could be full before their worst enemy, the buzzard, was up and about.

Fritz came up with an idea of nibbling away at the red and white stakes. But they soon all got toothache, as the markers turned out to be made of metal!

Suddenly **Fritz** disappeared. He had another idea – **Bruno** could help!

Deep under the roots of the oak lived a large family of rabbits who had built a complex tunnel system over the years. **Fritz** had visited **Bruno** many times, and usually knew where to find him. The rabbits were already up and about and listened carefully to the terrible news that **Fritz** had to tell. **Fritz** asked them if they could help by digging up the metal stakes.

In no time everyone was hard at work and **Balthazar**, who had been looking for **Fritz**, was very proud of his great-grandchild.

The two curious jays quickly noticed that there was something very special happening and sat down on the oak to watch. There, they harassed *Lou* until she explained to them what was going on. At the end she said, "OK you two, split up and go to the edge of the forest and make sure that the fox doesn't wreak havoc down there; the rabbits are too busy digging to look after themselves."

It wasn't long before the first jay reported back that the fox was on his way. Everyone sounded the alarm, and the rabbits and mice disappeared into their holes.

The fox was very upset, of course, as he now had to go right to the other end of the forest to catch his breakfast.

Under the protection of the watchful jays, the survey markers were dug up by mid-afternoon. Completely exhausted, **Fritz** disappeared into the safety of his hole to catch up with his sleep. He needed to be fully rested for the midnight meeting with the tree spirits! But he couldn't get to sleep, as he was too excited, not to mention scared, about the journey that awaited him.

The tree spirits were also restless. **Lou** flew once again over the tops of the trees and called loudly to everyone to come. The restlessness spread to all the animals in the forest who were awake and out hunting.

The weasels, for example, were quite curious and decided do go to the midnight meeting; the bats did likewise.

Shortly before midnight, **Fritz** and **Balthazar** waited anxiously in front of the old oak. How on earth were they going to get to the clearing in the forest and back safely?

But then, out floated **Big Cloud** from his tree hole to reassure them. When he saw the frightened faces of the two mice he said "What's up with you two? I think I need to bolster up your courage!"

And then he jumped up and started dancing around the oak and singing with that deep voice of his:

The tree spirits' tune

"Well, we'd better go now. We mustn't be late. Sit down on the two big leaves there and I will carry you on my shoulders."

He made himself so small and flat that he disappeared under the leaves. Then he inflated himself so that **Fritz** and **Balthazar** were gently lifted off the ground. They were still open-mouthed with amazement as they drifted towards the forest.

High over the tops of the trees they went until the clearing appeared below them.

From their vantage point they could see all the assembled tree spirits gleaming white in the moonlight. Then **Big Cloud** landed on a raised stone, shrank himself down to size so that **Fritz** and **Balthazar** could disembark from their leaves, and sit down beside him.

The tree spirits greeted **Big Cloud** with an eerie "Hoooo Hoooo Hoooo", whereupon **Big Cloud** inflated himself to an enormous size and made his eyes shine with a greenish light.

When everyone had finally settled down, **Big Cloud** greeted the tree spirits, explaining the reason for the meeting and why he had brought **Fritz** and **Balthazar** with him.

Fritz was now allowed to tell the large gathering all about his experiences. Then *Balthazar* explained that they must all stick together if they wanted to foil the humans' plans.

Fritz's report was so detailed that the witching hour was soon almost over. It was decided, that the bats should watch over the oak at night and the jays during the day. ***Lou***, who had been sitting on a branch nearby the entire time, also promised to continue helping. -

And then, with another eerie "Hoooo Hoooo Hoooo", the meeting came to a close. ***Fritz*** and ***Balthazar*** climbed back on their leaves and ***Big Cloud*** carried them home the way they had come.

While **Big Cloud** quickly fell asleep, those in the mouse hole stayed up and carried on the discussion. Outside the bats did their rounds. But all they saw were the weasels, who had secretly attended the meeting, sneaking home.

Early the next morning the jays raised the alarm. The jeep was back. This time the planning boss was alone in it, but he was followed by a heavy flat-bed truck with a bulldozer on it.

While the jays flew away, muttering to themselves, **Fritz** crept out of his hole and listened to the planning boss swearing about the unearthed survey makers and telling the truck driver to unload the bulldozer, but not yet start work as the stakes were not in place.

The jeep and the flat-bed truck disappeared again. But the silence didn't last long. Later in the afternoon the jeep returned, this time with the surveyor and her assistant.

The surveyor was amazed to see the unearthed stakes. She noticed the many rabbit tracks, but her assistant laughed when she pointed them out. "You don't honestly believe that rabbits dug up those survey markers, do you? It must have been some kids". The surveyor made no comment, but she knew she hadn't seen any human footprints. They got to work, measured out the road again and replaced all the stakes.

After the two had driven away, **Fritz** rushed back to his family to report what he had seen.

Once again **Fritz** was sent to **Bruno** and his rabbit family to have the stakes dug up again. And once again the jays watched over the area. But this time the fox didn't come, as there was too much going on around the old oak for his liking.

This time the rabbits had to work a lot harder, as the stakes had been driven even deeper into the ground. Night fell, but fortunately the moonlight was bright enough for them to see by.

The next afternoon the driver of the bulldozer returned. When he saw all the markers lying on the ground, he telephoned the boss, who drove the jeep back to the site, bringing with him the surveyor and her assistant. They assured him that they had put all the markers back the day before. Finally he believed them, even though the perpetrators had left no noticeable footprints.

The surveyor noticed the rabbit tracks once again, but didn't dare say anything for fear of being laughed at. Once again the humans set to work, and by nightfall the survey markers were all in place again. But it was far too late to begin work with the bulldozer.

It was decided that the driver of the bulldozer would come back the next day and that someone would guard the site overnight.

They drove away in the jeep, and a little later another car arrived with a different man inside, who stood guard for the night. First he looked over the entire area, at last he parked the car in such a way that he could easily watch over the bulldozer and the survey markers.

Once again **Fritz** had seen everything, and he reported it to **Balthazar**, who immediately rushed to **Big Cloud** to discuss the situation with him. What could they do against a bulldozer?

While they were turning the problem over and over in their minds, the bat that lived in **Big Cloud**'s hole spoke up and suggested that they ask the weasels for help. **Big Cloud** and **Balthazar** looked at him in amazement. The bat explained that he had seen the weasels secretly attending the meeting of the tree spirits, and that they must know what was going on.
The bat was sent with some of his friends to look for the weasels and warn them.
Dusk had fallen as the bats started their search for the weasels. They had no success until they came across some of the tree spirits, who were having a conversation in the big clearing.

One who lived at the edge of the forest had just seen the weasels. Quickly the new situation was explained to them, and the search continued until they finally found the weasel family. The bat flew back to report to **Big Cloud**.

Meanwhile, the security guard had made another round at dusk and hadn't noticed anything in particular. He had seen swathes of mist moving back and forth at the edge of the forest, but he had no idea that these were the tree spirits who were looking for the weasels along with the bats. He made himself comfortable in his car, turned on his car radio and listened to loud music to stay awake.

When the bat arrived back in the big oak tree, **Big Cloud** wanted to know "What can the weasels do to help us?".
"Well, you know how much they like to chew rubber hoses and electric cables. There's plenty of that stuff in the bulldozer, and if they want, there's even more in the guard's car!"

"Well, why didn't you say so before? That's a great idea! But now we have to get the weasels to the right place. You fly to the edge of the forest and get the tree spirits to drift over here slowly like clouds of mist. If the weasels stay underneath, they can get to the bulldozer without being seen, even though the moonlight is so bright tonight. The tree spirits should wrap themselves around the bulldozer so that the weasels can get to work. I'll l lie down over the guard's car so that the sneakiest weasel can start working very quietly on the engine cables. If the guard leaves the loud music on, he may not hear all the nibbling and gnawing."

The bat flew back to the edge of the forest and explained the plan to the tree spirits and weasels. They thought it was a great idea, and carefully set off for the oak tree. The guard could see swathes of mist moving slowly but surely from the edge of the forest across the meadow and towards the old oak.

Finally the cloud covered the entire area between the oak tree and the bulldozer, so that only the roof of the cabin and its exhaust pipe stuck out of it.

"Damn!" thought the guard. "Now, how am I supposed to keep watch? I can't see a thing!" He got out of his car to make a quick round of the survey markers. When he tried to get back, he could hardly find his car in the dense cloud of fog.

Irritated, he got in and convinced himself that because of the fog no-one would come and disturb the construction site.

Naturally he had no idea that **Big Cloud** had settled on his car like fog, or that there was a weasel nibbling away at the cables and hoses under the hood.

Inside the bulldozer, the weasels were chopping away happily. -

Later the rabbits joined them and tried to dig up the stakes again, but they were still quite tired from the work of the previous two nights and they had to admit that this time the stakes were driven very deep into the hard ground.

They couldn't finish the job and finally gave up at dawn with just a few holes at the base of the markers to show for their efforts.

Towards morning the security guard finally nodded off, and so he never noticed the weasels and tree spirits disappearing back into the night.

Big Cloud could finally breathe out, shrink himself down and retire to his tree hole.

Meanwhile the security guard got out of his car, yawned loudly and stretched. He then made a round of the site, but he noticed nothing except a few freshly dug rabbit holes in the ground. All he had to do now was to wait for the driver of the bulldozer.

He unpacked his breakfast and sat down with the door of his car open to enjoy the morning. Dewdrops were glistening on the blades of grass in the first rays of the morning sun. It was going to be a beautiful day.

Finally the bulldozer driver arrived in his car. They had known each other for ages, so they often joked with one another.

"So", the bulldozer driver winked at the guard. "Did you keep a good eye on those stakes?"
"Yeah", the guard yawned. "What a stupid job! And there was a ton of fog! Man, I'm dog tired! Look, you must make sure you don't drive over those stakes when you are coming round that tree, OK? But you know what? I still don't understand why they didn't cut the thing down right from the start. They have to get rid of it anyway."

"Maybe they don't have planning permission yet and want to start excavating just to put pressure on the planning department."

"Whatever! I just want to go home now. I'll see you later. And with that the guard got back into his car and put the key into the ignition. He turned the key again and again, but try as he might, the car would not start.

"We'll take care of that", said the bulldozer driver. "Open up the hood."?

They both stared at the engine and saw that the cables and hoses were badly damaged.

"What's been going on? You were keeping watch all night, weren't you? Didn't you hear anything?"
"No! I was listening to music to stay awake, dammit! Can you lend me your car until this afternoon? We can tow my car away when you have finished work. That way I can save some money on the towing charges."

"No problem! Just go ahead and take it. I don't need my car here anyway."

Meanwhile, **Fritz** had emerged from his hole and scurried under the car of the security guard. First he ate some of the crumbs from the guard's breakfast. While he ate, he listened intently to their conversation.

As the security guard drove off, he watched the bulldozer driver walk along the survey markers towards his machine.

He was eager to see what was going to happen with the bulldozer, because he knew from the rabbits what the weasels and tree spirits had accomplished the night before.

Carefully he followed the driver of the bulldozer and watched him climb in behind the steering wheel and put the key into the ignition.

The engine sprang to life. **Fritz** was shocked. Hadn't the weasels done their job properly? The bulldozer drove to the start of the line of stakes.

Jack and **Cracker**, the jays, and **Lou** the owl had heard the noise and raised the alarm. But what could the animals do against the bulldozer?

But the bulldozer driver was in for a surprise. When he tried to drive the shovel into the ground, nothing moved. He tried again and again, but without success. He got out of his cab and checked the hydraulic system that operated the shovel.

The weasels had done it! All the main hydraulic hoses had holes in them, and the oil was draining out.
The driver shook his head in amazement. "The animals seem to be against our roadworks!" he thought to himself.

What was he supposed to do now? He couldn't do any excavation work and he had lent his car to his friend, his handy in it. Maybe he should try hitchhiking home. But probably no-one would stop and pick him up on the open road, right on a bend. So he just decided to wait for his friend to return with his car.

He made himself comfortable under the old oak tree and began to look at his natural surroundings. For a second he thought that he had seen a fox at the edge of the forest.
Yes, it was definitely hunting mice. He watched, fascinated.

Above him *Jack* and *Cracker* had landed on a branch. They let some droppings fall right next to the driver. He looked up and grinned to them. "Ha! Ha! You missed!" he said. But he didn't move, as a group of mice had just gathered in front of him.

Before long, the rabbit family had also emerged from their burrow to look for food. The driver was astonished to discover how much life there was around the old oak.

Meanwhile the sun was rising higher in the sky, and it was becoming pleasantly warm. The driver made himself even more comfortable, and soon fell asleep under the oak tree.

Several hours later he awoke to find his friend staring at him.
"Now that's what I call digging, man!" he laughed.
"What's up with you? Not feeling well?"
"Oh, I´m fine. But the bulldozer isn't. The weasels not only ruined your car, they even managed to destroy the hydraulic cables. Nothing works anymore!"

"Well, something's definitely wrong with this site. Seems like the road won't get built after all." The bulldozer driver replied, "You know what? While

I was asleep I had a really strange dream. There was a little mouse here under the tree who was talking to a rabbit about the roadworks. They were congratulating the weasels on their good work and talking about what else they could do to stop us digging. If you hadn't woken me up," he laughed," I would probably found out what they are planning to do next!"

"Hey, hey, hold on now! Do you really believe in dreams? The bulldozer needs to be repaired, that's all. And then the road finally gets built. The boss is already furious. He'll go nuts when he hears about this latest setback."

Both of them drove away with the bulldozer driver's car, the guard's car in tow. Soon after, they came back with the flat-bed truck, loaded the bulldozer onto it and disappeared back to the garage.

Fritz had taken careful notes, and he rushed straight to *Balthazar* to explain what he had seen. One thing was for sure: the bulldozer would soon come back repaired.

It was true that, while the bulldozer driver had been asleep, *Fritz* had been talking to *Bruno* about what they could do to stop the roadworks, exactly as the driver had dreamt it!
Just as the guard had woken the driver, *Bruno* said to *Fritz*: "We need a new plan right now for fighting the humans away ourselves."
"Easier said than done! But, what if we ask the wasps? There's a wasp's nest in the old oak tree. But who dares go in there?"

Fritz promised to ask the wise *Balthazar*. On the way there he became more and more upset about the deep tracks the bulldozer and the flat-bed truck had left behind in the meadow.

Balthazar listened to the latest news. He thought the wasp idea was great, as he had often seen humans running away from wasps. But who dared visit the wasps in their nest to ask them? "***Big Cloud*** is the only one who can, and I am sure he will," said ***Balthazar***. "I will go to him right away!"

The old tree spirit had, of course, sensed what was going on and had heard all the noise of the cars and trucks.

"You've done a great job!" said ***Big Cloud*** once he had heard ***Balthazar***'s report. "Of course I would be glad to speak with the wasps. You know that they can't sting me, and I have always been curious as to what the inside of their nest looks like." ***Balthazar*** thanked him politely and bid him good day.

Big Cloud knew about the wasps' nest, of course, because it had been built in another corner of the partly hollow tree trunk. He also knew the wasps' routine, and so he waited until the evening when the air was cooler and they were back home.

He hovered over the entrance, made himself very small, and then slipped inside. The wasp guard at the entrance tried to stop him, but of course he could do nothing to stop a tree spirit. The wasps were soon in an uproar, and it was a while before **Big Cloud** could say "I have an urgent message for your Queen that is vitally important for all of you!"

A messenger was sent to the Queen to ask if she would grant an audience to the old tree spirit. The messenger soon returned with the information that yes, the Queen would receive the tree spirit. **Big Cloud** was immediately escorted to her.

The Queen sat enthroned on a slightly raised edge of a honeycomb. The yellow stripes of her armour were obviously freshly cleaned and glowed like gold in the dim light.

Big Cloud approached her with courtesy and respect, his tiny shrunken body glowing a soft green.

The Queen spoke. "Sir Tree Spirit, I see that you have come here in peace and friendship, but what is it exactly that brings you here to disturb the quiet of our evening?"

"Honourable Queen and neighbour," began ***Big Cloud***'s well-prepared speech. "First allow me to introduce myself. I am your neighbour and was already living in this old oak tree in the days when your great-grandmother laid her eggs in this place and ruled wisely over her subjects. My friends call me ***Big Cloud***. Usually my body is considerably larger than it is at the moment. Since I usually come out during the night, you have probably never seen me before, although we live so near to each other in this old oak."

"Thank you Sir for your introduction, but please come to the point", replied the Queen. "My people need to rest!"

"I will tell you my message right away. Your nest is in great danger. The humans want to cut down our oak and build a road through here."

The Queen and her subjects sat spellbound as *Big Cloud* recounted the previous events and told of the impending return of the bulldozer. *Big Cloud* then watched as the Queen of the wasps prepared her subjects for the great task at hand and assigned them their responsibilities. Guards, always accompanied by a messenger, would be positioned at fixed observation points on the road, its surroundings and around the old oak tree. Then, rest would be prescribed until dawn.

Big Cloud thanked the Queen for her help and bid her farewell, then set off in the direction of the clearing to continue discussing the plans.

The tree spirits were quickly called to the meeting. **Lou** the owl helped to fetch them and finally everybody was there. **Big Cloud** spoke about the plan with the wasps and said that, although he had expected the wasps to win, **Fritz** had found out that the works boss was still planning to cut down the old oak the next day. And whoever cut down the tree was sure to wear a protective suit against wasps.

They discussed the problem back and forth without success, until a very young tree spirit piped up.
"There must be a way to hide the tree!"

The suggestion brought a roar of laughter. But **Lou** the owl interrupted them. **Big Cloud** quieted everyone down by making his eyes glow, and then motioned **Lou** to continue her speech.

"We could ask the spiders to spin a dense blanket of cobwebs to cover the tree. And what's more, most people are afraid of spiders!" Of course a few spiders were at the clearing too, and they were asked if they could accomplish such a thing and if they wanted to help.

At first the spiders had their doubts, but eventually they agreed. But they would only help if everyone took part and they were given protection against spider-eating birds along the lengthy trail to the old oak.

Big Cloud and ***Lou*** agreed to organize that. Now all the spiders in the forest had to be informed about the plan. The weasel family volunteered to do the job.

The plan was for all the spiders in the forest to gather in the thicket during the course of the day. In the evening the tree spirits would guard the way to the oak by blowing themselves up into clouds of fog, under which the spiders could crawl there unseen.

The weasels made their way through the forest inch by inch to inform all the spiders. By morning they were done.

All day you could have watched the most astonishing trail of spiders moving in total silence, mostly under cover of leaves and branches. By late afternoon all of them were assembled at the edge of the forest opposite the oak.

Jack and ***Cracker*** flew a patrol at the edge of the forest to drive away any spider-eating birds.

Meanwhile, the humans too were having a discussion. The boss had indeed been extremely annoyed when the bulldozer driver had reported the damage done by the weasels. Naturally he blamed the security guard. His excuse was that he couldn't see anything because of the fog. The surveyor could contain herself no longer. "It seems to me that the animals there are fighting against our plan. When I saw all the rabbit tracks round the dug-up stakes, I thought that must be the explanation, but I didn't dare say so. You would have ridiculed me!"

"Oh, please! Don't talk such nonsense!" the boss interrupted. The security guard and the bulldozer driver tried to take the surveyor's side, but the boss would not listen.

By morning the bulldozer was expected to be repaired. "Tomorrow I will personally drive out there with you to make sure that the work gets done", the boss declared. "The day after tomorrow that oak is coming down. We will get permission from the planning department tomorrow."

The next morning promised a glorious warm day. **Jack** and **Cracker** took up their positions at the top of the oak and cleaned their feathers. They noticed that the messenger wasps were constantly hurrying back from the roadworks site, slipping into the nest and then flying back out again.

Late in the night, **Balthazar** had talked to **Big Cloud** and explained the new plan to **Fritz**.
Fritz now knew that an exciting day lay ahead, and he looked for a safe place from which he could watch everything easily.

Meanwhile the messengers announced that the flat-bed truck with the bulldozer had arrived, and so had the boss in the jeep. The wasps waited patiently as the bulldozer was off-loaded. Then the flat-bed drove away.

The watchmen were flying so high that the two humans failed to notice them. After every updates the Queen smiled with satisfaction, but she simply said, "Keep waiting!"

The fighters were already impatient, but they soon understood why they were having to wait. The boss and the bulldozer driver walked along the construction site, went over the plans for the roadwork again and decided where they would put the excavated earth.

It was by now quite hot, so the bulldozer driver and his boss took off their jackets and shirts. The driver climbed into the bulldozer's cab and rolled down the windows.

The boss found himself a nice sunny spot and made himself comfortable. He blinked contentedly into the warm sun.

The bulldozer engine was now roaring away so loudly that neither the driver nor his boss heard danger approaching.

The bulldozer had just started its work when the attack began. The leaders of the squadrons ordered their fighters to sting the hands, faces and backs of the bulldozer driver and his boss, all at the same time.

The two panicked. The driver thought that he could escape in the bulldozer and raced across the meadow, flattening most of the survey markers in the process. He finished unhappily by ramming into the boss's jeep. He jumped out of the cab and ran in the direction of the motorway with wasps swarming around him.

The boss tried to save himself by jumping into his jeep, almost getting flattened by the rampaging bulldozer as he ran. His eyes were beginning to swell and he could just see the bulldozer smashing into his car.

What could he do now except run away from the wasps in the direction of the motorway? The wasps followed him and refused to leave him alone until he reached the edge of the road.

Both men were now frantically waving their arms at the side of the road, hoping someone would come. Luckily for them, a driver stopped and took them both straight to the hospital when he saw what had happened to them.

The wasps returned to their nest and were rewarded with sweet nectar. Some of them were missing, however: they had been killed in the attack. Others had bent wings or legs. Several had broken stings.

The Queen nursed them and praised the fighters for their great victory.

Fritz had seen everything and quickly fetched ***Balthazar*** so that he could tell him how successful his idea had been.

In the hospital, the bulldozer driver and his boss were being treated with a series of injections and infusions until they were out of danger. Their faces, hands and backs were terribly swollen, so much that they couldn't lie down properly and rest, even though they were exhausted.
The bulldozer driver sat muttering to himself. From time to time he mumbled, "I told you the animals were fighting back", while the boss growled over and over again, "That tree has got to go, that tree has got to go!"

By the next morning they both felt a little better. The boss got somebody to drive him to his office, hoping to get the oak tree felled right away. But he had no idea what ***Big Cloud*** had in store for him.
The spiders had started their trek across the meadow to the oak while the works boss and

the bulldozer driver were treated in the hospital. Car drivers on the nearby motorway wondered about the clouds of fog that were drifting across the forest to the big oak, but they had no idea that it was the tree spirits covering the spiders' path in mist. Finally the old oak tree itself disappeared into the fog.

Would the spiders really be able to make a whole oak tree disappear behind a curtain of cobwebs?

Next morning a heated, even furious discussion broke out in the boss's office. The surveyor had suggested giving up the roadbuilding project. The boss, his face still red and swollen with wasp stings, disagreed and flew into rage.

"Call the forester right away, and let's get this oak cut down!" was the one thought in his mind. The surveyor had to take her boss in her car and pick up the forester and his chainsaw. She then drove the two of them to the site.

The jays, *Jack* and *Cracker*, spotted the car on the road long before it arrived on the scene, and they warned the tree spirits, who were already prepared. They drifted out to the road and positioned themselves so that the surveyor had to drive very slowly and carefully in her car. The spiders had still not quite finished their work.

There was by now dense fog, especially where the car was to turn from the road onto the meadow. Consequently the surveyor missed the turn and had to do a lengthy detour before she could turn back. Needless to say, her boss flew into another rage.

Finally they located the turnoff and drove into the meadow where, in the fog, they found the bulldozer and the boss's dented jeep.

The oak was, so dense was the fog, invisible. They got out of the car and walked gingerly the rest of the way while the forester prepared his chainsaw. Suddenly the surveyor screamed.

She had walked into a wall of cobwebs and was covered from head to toe in them. She tried to pull herself away and then saw to her amazement that she was standing in front of an immense cobweb curtain, in which she had ripped a hole. And behind the curtain was the oak.

Her scream had alerted the boss, who came over to inspect the extraordinary cobweb curtain. He stood there aghast.

"Isn't it time to give up?" the surveyor urged. "Can't you see how all the animals are fighting to save their tree?"
"No! I won't give up!" the boss yelled. "This makes me all the more determined to get rid of it!" He shouted to the forester to go ahead and cut down the tree.

The forester was also standing dumbfounded in front of the cobweb curtain and staring at it as if it was the eighth wonder of the world.

Hesitantly he obeyed the boss's order, the chainsaw in his hands. As he prepared to cut into the trunk he noticed that the ground around him was swarming with spiders. He suddenly felt spiders crawling up his legs inside his pants. He started shaking himself, and as he did so the running chain saw touched the ground. He slipped, fell and hit his leg with the saw.

The boss had stood paralyzed as he watched the accident. Now he ran over to the forester. They helped him to the surveyor's car. The wound was bleeding badly, even though it didn't seem very deep.
As they bandaged the forester, the boss sighed and finally said! I give up! If we go ahead, there'll be an even bigger disaster here. The animals have won! They can keep their old oak. I'll suggest a change of plan. We'll keep the bend in the road and build a nice picnic area here beside the old tree."

The surveyor agreed enthusiastically. – Meanwhile the forester was recovering from the shock. Together they watched in total amazement as the dense fog disappeared and formed a strip between the old oak and the edge of the forest.

On the ground they discovered an unbelievable number of spiders who were creeping back into the forest under the ribbon of fog.

The old oak remained, covered in the blanket of cobwebs. As they were driving back into town to get medical attention for the forester's wound, they realized that this would be a moment that they would never forget.

As usual, **Fritz**, the little mouse, had observed everything from his hiding-place and had even overheard the conversation.
Big Cloud was relieved when he could finally breathe out again. It had been a huge effort for him to stay blown up so big for so long, big enough for the entire oak to disappear inside him.

When the spiders arrived at the edge of the forest, the other tree spirits could finally go home and get some rest as well.

Before doing so, though, they made an appointment to meet that evening under the old oak tree.

That same afternoon, workers came and picked up the bulldozer and the boss's dented jeep.

In the evening the surveyor drove back to the old oak tree. She parked the car at the side of the road and sat at the top of a gentle slope at the edge of the meadow.

She wanted to think about how to build a picnic area there that wouldn't disturb the harmony of nature. While she was sitting there as the sun set, a number of small clouds drifted out of the forest and across to the meadow under the oak tree. Then a foggy figure emerged from the Oak itself and floated into the middle of the other clouds, just as if the others were making room for it.

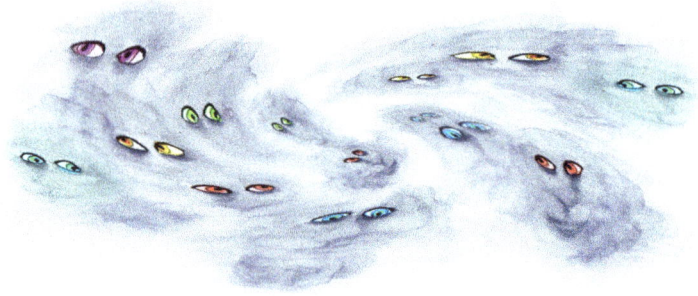

At one point she thought that she saw greenish lights – what people call o'the wisp. These were the eyes of the tree spirits as they twinkled merrily over and over again.

The surveyor noticed that she was humming a melody in time with the movements of the tree spirits. She suddenly felt at one with nature.

It was late in the evening when she finally got up and went back to her car deep in thought.

There is not much more to tell. The surveyor presented a plan for the picnic area that was accepted, and the picnic area was built with great care and consideration for the nature all around it.

The rabbit and mouse families had to rebuild part of their homes.

The next sunny day all of the animals celebrated a dancing party under the old oak.

Fritz and his family soon discovered that there were often delicious breadcrumbs and other delicacies to be found under the picnic tables.

Warning signs appeared on the road:

CAUTION!
FREQUENT FOG PATCHES!

So what do people know about tree spirits?

Bodo Henningsen

Milton Keynes UK
Ingram Content Group UK Ltd.
UKHW020801110224
437528UK00010BA/99